The Plastic Problem

A boy sifts through waste polluting the Ci Liwung river in Java, Indonesia, looking to collect valuable plastic.

Contents

Introduction

Plastic is everywhere. We sit on it. We stand on it. We drink from it. We eat from it. We are obsessed with it. But why?

Well, we need lots of stuff to help us live our lives the way that we do. We need cars, busses and trains to get around; we need houses and apartments to live in; and we need containers to hold all of our stuff. Plastic is a miracle material when it comes to many of these things. When compared with metal, glass or wood, plastic is often cheaper to manufacture and is a more versatile product. It can be firm or soft, it can be molded into any shape and it is one of the most durable materials on the planet.

With characteristics like these, you think plastic would be considered very valuable — almost precious! Unfortunately, 40% of this amazing material is wasted on packaging that is designed to be used once and then thrown away. You likely interact with these items daily — things such as soda bottles, plastic bags and bubble wrap (although popping bubble wrap *is* very fun). Most often this waste finds its way into a landfill or is burned up in an incinerator. Sometimes, if it's lucky, it gets recycled. But, more often than not, it finds its way into the environment. In fact, the equivalent of one garbage truck full of plastic waste is dumped into the ocean every minute. It is a staggering amount.

Our ocean is drowning in plastic! We must save it if we want to have a future on this planet. The first step is to learn as much as possible about plastic, the problem we face with it and the possible solutions we can try.

In this book we investigate how plastic is made, how it travels to the seas and how it impacts millions of animals. We will also look at ways in which people are turning the tide on plastic pollution and how even you can make an impact in this global crisis.

Let's not delay. The plastic problem is real. Read on, and together we can be a part of the solution!

Plastic, plastic everywhere! Times Square in New York City couldn't look like this without it.

What is Plastic?

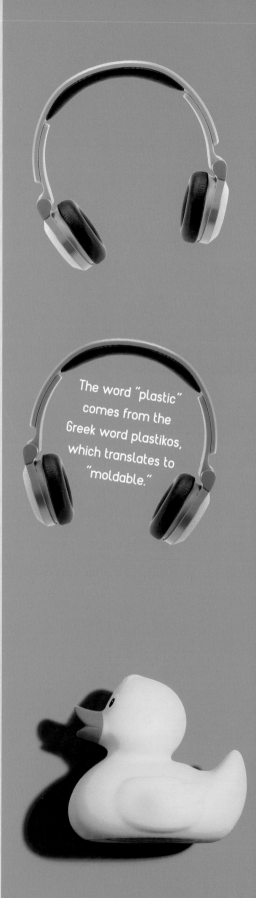

The word "plastic" comes from the Greek word plastikos, which translates to "moldable."

Different types of plastic can look and feel very differently. For example, your bike helmet has a hard plastic shell, but plastic fibers in a sweater can be soft, even fuzzy. A rubber duck made of plastic can float, but a nylon fishing rope will sink. Plastic can be thin, like the plastic wrap you use to cover food, or thick, like playground equipment. It can be flexible, like a garden hose, or stiff, like a video game controller. With all of these different features, it makes you wonder, what exactly is plastic?

FROM ONE TO MANY

Each type of plastic is remarkably unique, but they all have one thing in common: They are made of large molecules called polymers. Polymers are made of lots of tiny molecules called monomers. Let's look at how these two words are formed:

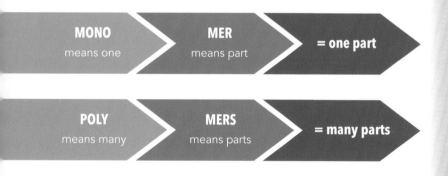

MONO means one	MER means part	= one part

| POLY means many | MERS means parts | = many parts |

Think of one paper clip as a single monomer. Then think of a pile of paper clips as a bunch of monomers. Now link all of those paper clips together into a chain, and that is a polymer.

ONE PAPERCLIP

MANY PAPERCLIPS

PAPERCLIP CHAIN

ONE MONOMER

MANY MONOMERS

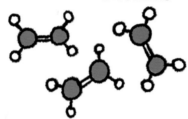

POLYMER

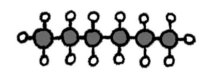

ETHYLENE

This monomer is made of two molecules of carbon and four molecules of hydrogen. Molecules can be represented with formulas, and the formula for ethylene is C_2H_4.

POLYETHYLENE

This polymer is made of many ethylene molecules, hence the name *poly*ethylene. Polyethylene is an important ingredient in many of the plastics you will learn about in this book.

Plastics are grouped into two main polymer families — thermoplastics and thermosets. Thermoplastics turn soft when heated and harden when cooled. Shampoo bottles, rubber ducks and garden hoses are good examples of thermoplastics. Thermosets, on the other hand, never turn soft once they have been molded. Milk crates and rigid car and aeroplane parts are examples of thermosets.

How Plastics are Made

Plastic is very much a human invention. However, there are also natural plastics. The Olmecs, people from ancient Mexico, created rubber from, well, rubber trees! Much later, in 1856, Alexander Parkes used wood cellulose — the material that makes branches and other plant parts firm but bendy — to make celluloid.

The very first synthetic plastic, bakelite, was invented in 1907. Named after inventor Leo Baekeland, it was the first ever plastic to be made from fossil fuels instead of plants or animals. Bakelite used phenol, which is an acid made from coal. And it is here, with the invention of bakelite, that we can start to understand how plastic is made today.

FROM A GAS TO A NURDLE

Making plastic requires a lot of work, especially because 99% of all plastic is made from fossil fuels, such as crude oil and natural gas. So in order to make everything from your headphones to your toothbrush, fossil fuels need to be dug out of the ground and refined and transformed.

DRILLING

Fossil fuels such as oil and gas can be taken from land or sea by drilling into the ground. Fossil fuels are formed by the decomposition of ancient plants and animals that were buried under sand and rock for centuries (these are fossils). The surrounding sand and rock created pressure and heat around the decaying plants and animals, which turned them into fuel. Oil companies drill holes into the Earth's crust, creating a well, and then pump the fuel out (as they are here in California). Oil wells can be drilled on land or in the middle of an ocean, through the seafloor.

REFINING

Refining removes things such as water, carbon dioxide and sulfide from the oil that has been pumped from underground. Crude oil is a thick, dark brown mixture of a bunch of different molecules. Heating crude oil separates all of the different molecules into layers.

CRACKING

This is a process that cracks or breaks molecules into smaller pieces. These smaller molecules are called monomers, which are the building blocks of plastic.

POLYMERIZATION

A catalyst — something that can speed up a chemical reaction — is added to the monomers, which makes them connect together, forming polymers. This process is called polymerization. There are a lot of different kinds of plastics, but the term that describes all of them is "polymers." At this stage, other chemicals are added to the plastic to change its characteristics. Some give the plastic bright colors, while others can make it more flexible or really stiff and strong.

NURDLES

The polymerized liquid is cooled and chopped into tiny pieces. These pieces are called "nurdles." Nurdles are 1/32 to 1/4 inch (1 to 5 mm) in size. The dots here represent 5/64 inch (2 mm) nurdles. Nurdles are shipped around the world and are used to make thousands of different things.

ENVIRONMENTAL IMPACTS

The drilling and transportation of crude oil and natural gas can lead to spills like the one pictured here in Koh Samet, Thailand. These spills can impact our drinking water and harm — even kill — animals.

Fifty percent of natural gas is extracted by a process called fracking. Chemicals, sand and water are injected at a very high pressure directly into rock. This process cracks open the rock and releases the gases trapped inside, which are then pumped out. This can lead to groundwater contamination. Scientists are also concerned that fracking might lead to more earthquakes, since it disturbs bedrock (the rock that lies at the bottom of the soil and other materials that make up the ground we walk on).

The process of transforming various molecules into plastic products can release a lot of toxins into our atmosphere. Additionally, it can create liquid waste that can flow into our rivers, lakes and oceans.

The people who make plastic are also affected. Scientists have found that during the heating process, plastics can release toxins that are linked to cancer. They have even found that making plastic can change your DNA if you are not properly protected!

MAKING THINGS WITH PLASTIC

How does a collection of tiny nurdles transform into something we recognize, like a cup or a Frisbee? Manufacturers using plastic apply heat to the nurdles to turn them into the consistency of modeling clay. They then inject the hot plastic into molds. (Molds that can have material injected into them are called "injectable molds.") The plastic hardens as it cools, and it is then pushed out of the mold. The process then starts all over again! Plastic can be heated and cooled much more quickly than most materials, which means plastic is very easy to mold. This is one of the reasons why plastic goods are so cheap to make. Plastic can be molded into almost any shape very quickly. It is also much lighter than many other materials. Therefore, shipping a barrel of nurdles around the globe is a lot cheaper than shipping a large steel coil or logs of wood. The materials used to make plastic are also quite cheap to buy. One of the big reasons why plastic is everywhere is because it keeps production costs very low.

Over 343 million tons (311 million metric tons) of plastic are produced each year. That's the weight of more than 900 Empire State Buildings!

LOTS OF LEGO

LEGO has perfected plastic manufacturing. They heat nurdles of ABS plastic (acrylonitrile butadiene styrene) and inject it into molds in the shape of a particular brick. LEGO factories don't just have one mold — there are lots of molds! LEGO makes over 1,000 pieces per second, meaning they make about 36 billion pieces every year!

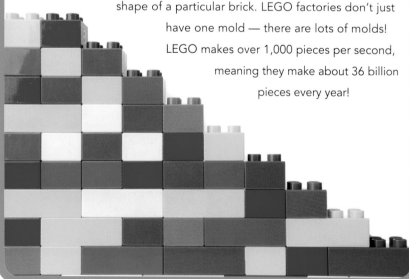

Plastic at Home

How many things do you live with that are made of plastic? Try this: Tomorrow morning, when you wake up, try counting all of the plastic items you touch. During my morning routine, I interact with 37 plastic objects in the first 20 minutes I'm awake.

Most people have a lot of plastic in their homes — and a lot of different types, too! The names of these plastics are long and sometimes difficult to pronounce. Those names, as hard as they are to say, describe the kinds of chemicals added to change the structure, shape, feel and purpose of the particular plastic. Here are some different types:

POLYMETHYL METHACRYLATE (PMMA)

is used to make a substitute for glass that is shatterproof, meaning it's much harder to break. This material can be so strong that it is bulletproof! PMMA is also used to make acrylic paint.

POLYBUTYLENE TEREPHTHALATE (PBT)

Did you know that most cars are 8% plastic? One of those plastics is PBT. This strong plastic can withstand heavy impacts, such as a car crash. Therefore, a car bumper made of PBT helps keep the driver and passengers safe.

POLYETHYLENE TEREPHTHALATE (PET)

is one of the world's most common plastics. It can be made into fibers for clothing, furniture and carpeting. It is also used for food packaging.

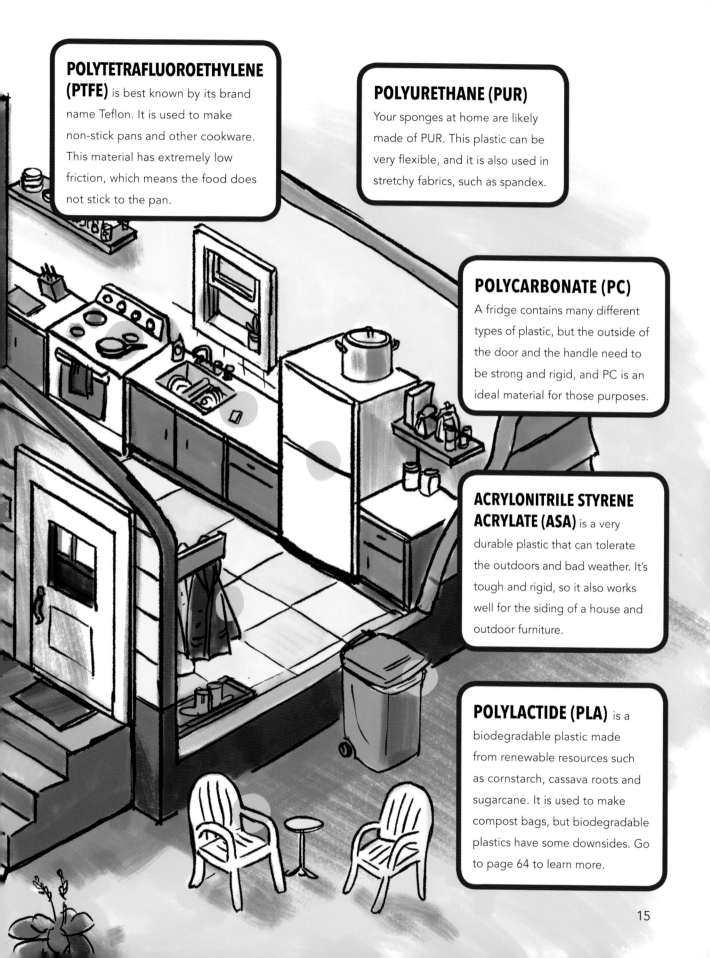

POLYTETRAFLUOROETHYLENE (PTFE) is best known by its brand name Teflon. It is used to make non-stick pans and other cookware. This material has extremely low friction, which means the food does not stick to the pan.

POLYURETHANE (PUR) Your sponges at home are likely made of PUR. This plastic can be very flexible, and it is also used in stretchy fabrics, such as spandex.

POLYCARBONATE (PC) A fridge contains many different types of plastic, but the outside of the door and the handle need to be strong and rigid, and PC is an ideal material for those purposes.

ACRYLONITRILE STYRENE ACRYLATE (ASA) is a very durable plastic that can tolerate the outdoors and bad weather. It's tough and rigid, so it also works well for the siding of a house and outdoor furniture.

POLYLACTIDE (PLA) is a biodegradable plastic made from renewable resources such as cornstarch, cassava roots and sugarcane. It is used to make compost bags, but biodegradable plastics have some downsides. Go to page 64 to learn more.

Plastic in Our Groceries

RECYCLED POLYETHYLENE TEREPHTHALATE (RPET; RESIN CODE 1) When PET is recycled, that material can be broken down to make new things, such as this container for strawberries! Only clean PET can be melted down to make new products, which is why it's important to clean your containers before putting them in the recycling bin.

People often bring a lot of plastic home with them when they go to the grocery store. If you want to know the types of plastics that are used in a product's packaging, check the label. It is often stamped on the bottom of the container. This is known as the *Resin Identification Code.* For example, you might find this symbol on the bottom of a container of mints. The 5 stands for polypropylene, and it is also sometimes symbolized with PP. How many different codes can you find in your home?

HIGH-DENSITY POLYETHYLENE (HDPE; RESIN CODE 2) Single-use plastic bags, such as those used for groceries, are often made of HDPE, but so are things that are more sturdy, like yogurt containers.

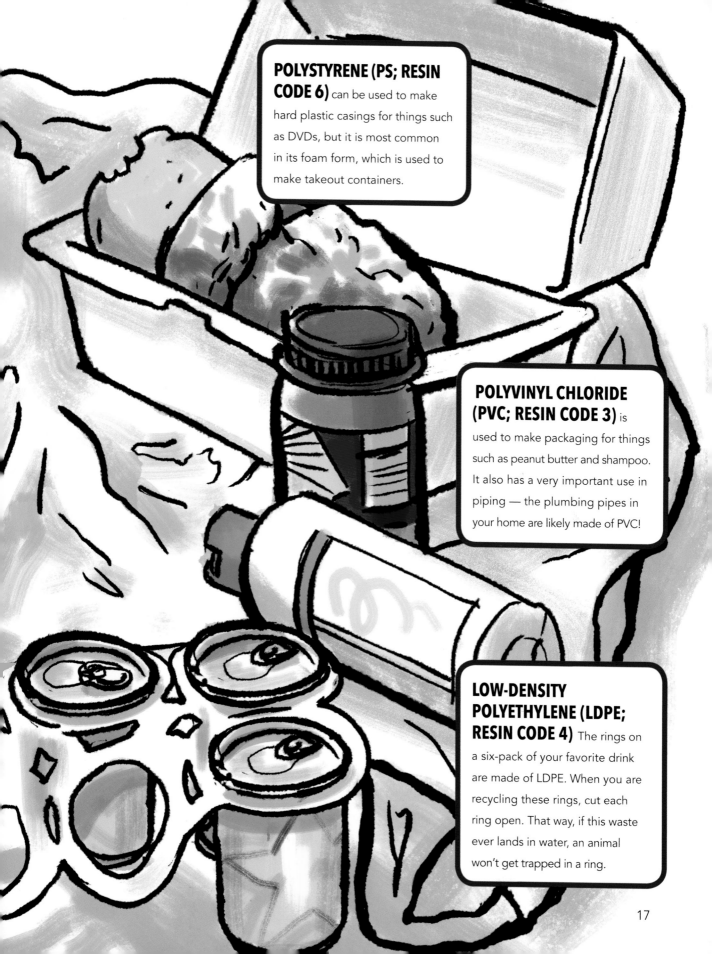

POLYSTYRENE (PS; RESIN CODE 6) can be used to make hard plastic casings for things such as DVDs, but it is most common in its foam form, which is used to make takeout containers.

POLYVINYL CHLORIDE (PVC; RESIN CODE 3) is used to make packaging for things such as peanut butter and shampoo. It also has a very important use in piping — the plumbing pipes in your home are likely made of PVC!

LOW-DENSITY POLYETHYLENE (LDPE; RESIN CODE 4) The rings on a six-pack of your favorite drink are made of LDPE. When you are recycling these rings, cut each ring open. That way, if this waste ever lands in water, an animal won't get trapped in a ring.

Lots of Plastic, Lots of Waste

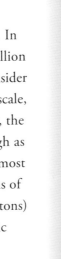

We have been mass-producing plastic for about 60 years. In this short time, we have created 9.1 billion tons (8.3 billion metric tons) of plastic! So how much is 9.1 billion tons? Consider this, if every person on the planet stood together on a giant scale, our combined weight would not come close to that. In fact, the world's population would have to grow by 26 times to weigh as much as the plastic we have produced! The problem is that most of that plastic ends up as waste. In fact, of the 9.1 billion tons of plastic we have created, 6.9 billion tons (6.3 billion metric tons) has wound up as waste. This means that 69% of all the plastic we've created has become garbage!

DIFFICULT TO RECYCLE

There are two main types of plastic: thermoplastics and thermosets. Thermoplastics are recyclable. They are easy to melt and turn into new objects. Thermosets are not recyclable. They will not melt no matter how much you heat them. These plastics are often incinerated, transforming them into ash, gas and heat.

WHERE DOES THE WASTE GO?

There are things made of plastic that we use for a long time before we throw them away, such as computers or scooters. But almost half of all the plastic we make is used for packaging, such as the bubble wrap pictured on this page. This packaging is often single use, meaning we use it once and then we throw it away. Every minute, people around the world throw away a total of 1 million plastic bottles and 9 million plastic bags. This plastic waste goes to a variety of places, but probably not where you think. So where does it go?

6.9 BILLION TONS OF PLASTIC

12% **79%** **9%**

INCINERATION

A total of 12% of plastic waste is incinerated. Incineration means destroying something by burning it. This method reduces the plastic waste to byproducts of ash, gas and heat. However, the act of incinerating plastic has harmful side effects, including greenhouse gas emissions that contribute to climate change and dioxin emissions, which are very toxic to both people and animals.

LANDFILL/NATURAL ENVIRONMENT

A total of 79% of plastic waste ends up in landfills. Plastic is designed to be durable and strong, which means it can take up to 1,000 years to decompose. All too often, plastic waste destined for the landfill ends up in the environment, and the majority of this enters our oceans. Scientists estimate that 8.8 million tons (8 million metric tons) make it into the oceans each year. This is equal to dumping a garbage truck's worth of trash into the oceans every minute.

RECYCLING

Unfortunately, only 9% of plastic is recycled. But why is this number so low? One reason is that a lot of plastic that is recyclable is put in the garbage instead of the recycling bin. In some communities a recycling plant may not be capable of recycling all types of plastic. Yet another reason plastic isn't recycled is that it's dirty. Any plastic with food residue on it cannot be recycled — so wash your plastic!

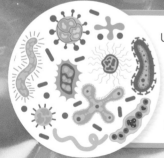

Until recently, it was thought that bacteria could not to eat plastic. However, in 2016 scientists discovered a type of bacteria named *Ideonella sakaiensis* that does eat plastic! Helped by a rare enzyme, which speeds up the degradation of plastic, this little fella is a bright spot in the ongoing plastic waste dilemma. However, *Ideonella sakaiensis* isn't a golden ticket to the end of all plastic waste!

PLASTIC IN LANDFILLS

Plastic in a landfill, like the one seen here in the Maldives, is a big problem because it stays there for centuries and can create nasty byproducts.

1,000 Years

In a landfill, wood, food scraps and other types of organic matter go through a process called biodegradation. This means microorganisms such as bacteria and fungi decompose the waste, turning it into other useful things, such as soil. But fungi and bacteria don't like to eat plastic, so the plastic doesn't biodegrade. Some plastic, like the plastic in a water bottle, can take 400 to 1,000 years to decompose!

Dangerous Leachate

As rain falls on a landfill, the water filters through the trash and absorbs stuff from it. If there is plastic in the landfill, the rainwater absorbs some of the chemicals used to make that plastic. Eventually, the rainwater leaks out from the landfill. When it does, it is called leachate. Leachate is full of chemicals and can be highly toxic if it seeps into our groundwater, soil and rivers.

Photodegradation

Photodegradation happens when the sun's UV rays break up the chains of polymers that make plastic. This makes the plastic brittle, and it begins to break into smaller pieces. But this plastic never truly goes away. Instead, it continues to break down until it is so small it turns into tiny microplastic. Microplastic is very easy for animals to eat, which causes many other problems.

FROM LAND TO SEA

How is plastic getting into our oceans by the truckload?

Lost in Production

Before plastic is turned into anything useable, it is a tiny nurdle. A nurdle is no bigger than this dot ●. Something this small is easy to lose. Have you ever poured a bag of beads or beans into a jar? Chances are you spilled some. The same thing happens to nurdles. However, over time millions of these nurdles enter our waterways each year.

Blown by the Wind

Plastic is very light, so when trash is overflowing in bins or landfills — and especially when it's littered on the ground — it can get picked up by the wind and blown into rivers. Additionally, when it rains, the litter on the ground gets carried into our sewer systems, which eventually drain into large bodies of water.

Rivers Flow to the Sea

Of the 8.8 million tons (8 million metric tons) of plastic that enter the oceans each year, about half comes from our rivers. However, rivers flowing through regions where waste management is poor or nonexistent end up contributing the most waste. For example, the Yangtze River in China adds 1.7 million tons (1.5 million metric tons) of plastic to the oceans each year! As a planet, if we want to fight the plastic crisis, we need to support these nations and help them build or improve their waste management systems.

From Coast to Corals

When glimpsed from space, the Earth looks predominantly blue. Why? Because our planet is mostly water — it is 71% water, to be precise. Of that water, 97% is found in our oceans, which have a landscape and ecology all their own. From the cold depths of the deep sea to the warm regions where coral reefs thrive, plastic pollution is having major consequences. If you were to take all of the waste dumped into the oceans each year and line it up along the shoreline, you would have five garbage bags of plastic for every foot of coastline in the world!

Coast

Plastic bottles, packaging, fishing buoys and other large items make for visual clutter, as they do here on the coast of Bunaken Island in Indonesia, but one of the most common waste items found on our coasts are cigarette butts. Some studies have found that cigarette butts can make up to 50% of shoreline waste. Smokers may toss their butts on the ground thinking that they will biodegrade, but this is not true. The filters in cigarettes are made of microplastic fibers that take a long time to biodegrade. The other main contributor to shoreline waste are microplastics that have washed ashore from the sea. For every 250 ml of sand or sediment there is an estimated 2–30 plastic particles across our coastlines.

Islands

Islands are not safe from plastic debris. Pictured here is Henderson Island — a small island in the south of the Pacific Ocean, where no people live. It has the highest density of plastic waste in the world. Scientists estimate that for every square foot of island, there are about 62 plastic items (or 671 plastic items per square meter of island).

On the Surface

A lot of plastic floats! Why? It's all about density! Density means how tightly or loosely the molecules that make up an object are packed together. If the plastic has a higher density than the seawater in which it is floating, it will sink; examples of plastics that sink are styrene and nylon. But polyethylene and polypropylene, which have a lower density than seawater, do float! This floating plastic can form giant patches of waste that bob along the ocean's surface.

Coral

Coral reefs are the nurseries of the sea. They provide essential habitat for millions of fish and other aquatic creatures, and they protect the shore by breaking up strong waves during powerful storms. Coral reefs are currently being threatened by climate change, and this threat is only made worse by plastic pollution.

When plastic lands on coral, it not only stresses the coral by blocking out the sunlight it needs to thrive, it can also infect the coral with bacteria. Plastic provides the perfect environment for some harmful bacteria to grow and travel, including *Vibrio coralliilyticus*, which can make coral develop the disease known as "White Syndrome." This mysterious disease leaves white stripes on the coral's surface, where it has killed the life that was once there. Scientists estimate that there are 11 billion plastic items on coral reefs across the Asia-Pacific region alone.

Traps

When it comes to fishing equipment, plastic can be found from the oceans' surface to the floor. For example, lobster traps are dropped to the bottom of the ocean, but in order for fishers to find them and retrieve them, these traps are connected to long plastic ropes and a floating buoy (which is a large object that floats at the surface of the water and serves as a marker). These traps, as well as fishing nets, provide many challenges for the animals that swim past them.

Mariana Trench

The Mariana Trench is the deepest point in the ocean. The maximum known depth is 36,070 feet (10,994 m). If you dropped Mount Everest into the trench, its peak would still be more than 1 mile (2 km) underwater! A place so deep and remote must be squeaky clean, right? Wrong. Divers have found plastic grocery bags even there.

Surprisingly, the Mariana Trench may have higher levels of pollution than the most polluted rivers in the world. A study found that persistent organic pollutant (POP) levels are very high in the trench. POPs likely got there by attaching themselves to plastic that was floating in the water and then collected at the bottom of the ocean. Even though a lot of plastic floats, eventually a lot of it sinks! A recent study predicts that 90% of microplastics will make their way to the ocean floor.

Deadly Debris

With plastic waste dotting every part of the planet, it is no wonder that more than 1,000 different animal species are harmed by our plastic pollution. Of those species, 700 are known to eat plastic, and millions of animals also become trapped and tangled in it. But plastic is most dangerous to animals in our oceans. Here are a few of the many species struggling to survive in waters full of our garbage.

RIGHT WHALES

Our plastic pollution could be most dangerous for right whales. There are only 411 North Atlantic Right Whales left on Earth, and in 20 years this giant mammal could be extinct. The number one cause of death for these whales, like the one pictured here, is getting tangled in fishing gear. Even when volunteers free whales from nets, the wounds can leave the whales at risk of infection.

These aren't the only type of whales affected by our plastic pollution. In 2019 a Cuvier's beaked whale was found dead in the Philippines with 88 pounds (40 kg) of plastic in its stomach, including plastic bags and fishing ropes. Similarly, a pilot whale died with 17 pounds (8 kg) of plastic waste inside its stomach, including 80 plastic bags.

A MAZE OF LINES AND NETS

The fishing industry creates a lot of plastic waste that ends up in our oceans. Commercial fishers use lines and nets to catch large quantities of fish and seafood, and they sometimes leave their nets and lines behind. These are known as "ghost nets," and they are left floating in the middle of the ocean. An estimated 700,000 tons (640,000 metric tons) of fishing gear is abandoned each year, and thousands of mammals and seabirds end up trapped in this maze of gear, resulting in injuries and even deaths.

SEABIRDS

Seabirds are considered indicators of the overall health of marine environments. With this in mind, we should be very concerned! Since the 1950s, seabird populations have decreased by 67%. Plastic has played a big role in these declines. In 1960, plastic was found in less than 5% of birds' stomachs, but today that number is 90%. The amount of plastic in bird bellies is even higher in places like Australia, South Africa and South America, where coastlines are close to patches of floating plastic.

What kind of plastic do birds eat? Common items include clothing fibers, bags, bottle caps and tiny plastic fragments worn down by waves and the sun. Sharp plastic can pierce a bird's internal organs or block its airway, so it can't breathe. But most often, a bird that eats plastic ends up with a stomach full of plastic that it can't digest. This can weigh it down, leaving it unable to fly. It also leaves no room in the bird's stomach for actual food, so many birds starve to death. Some seabirds are more affected by plastic than others:

CAN YOU TELL THE DIFFERENCE?

The photo on the top is a bunch of herring fish eggs. The photo on the bottom is a bunch of plastic nurdles. Now imagine you were a bird that didn't know what plastic was. Fish eggs are a huge part of many species' diets. When the two look so much alike, it's easy to see why animals eat so much plastic.

Laysan Albatross

These amazing birds (pictured here) have a wingspan of over 6 feet (1.8 m) and are known to stick with one mate their entire life. Laysan Albatross like to feed on fish and squid by skimming the surface of the water with their beak. This method of catching food leads them to accidentally scoop up a lot of plastic that's floating on the surface of the water. Adults will then feed what they have caught to their chicks. The chicks cannot throw up the plastic, so it fills their stomach. In Hawaii, 97% of Laysan Albatross chicks found dead had plastic in their stomach.

Flesh-footed Shearwater

The Flesh-footed Shearwater eats more plastic than any other marine bird and possibly more than any other marine animal. Like the Laysan Albatross, shearwaters feed close to the surface, and they pick up plastic when they mistake it for larvae or fish eggs. In one study, researchers found 276 pieces of plastic in a single bird, accounting for 14% of its body weight. This plastic can prevent the bird from properly digesting its food, but scientists have uncovered chemical effects, too. Plastics accumulate microscopic metals and pollutants on their surface, and when birds eat the plastic, these contaminants enter into the animal's blood stream. The more plastic the shearwaters ate, the higher the levels of contaminants they ingested — including the metal chromium, which is known to have neurotoxic effects.

SMELLS LIKE FOOD?

A lot of ocean plastic has algae growing on it. As the algae breaks down, it emits a stinky odor, which is a chemical called dimethyl sulfide. Birds, sea turtles, sharks and whales have learned to associate the smell of this chemical with food, so it's no wonder so many animals mistake plastic for a tasty meal. Researchers have found that the more a species likes this smell, the more plastic it eats.

SEA TURTLES

Sea turtles love snacking on jellyfish! Unfortunately, jellyfish and plastic bags can look a lot alike. This is bad news for turtles, as ingesting a bag can result in a stomach blockage. If a turtle has too much plastic in its stomach, it will have trouble digesting food, causing it to be malnourished or even to starve. If a turtle isn't getting proper nutrition, this will also disrupt the growth of its young. One study estimated that 52% of all sea turtles worldwide have eaten plastic debris.

Not only are turtles eating plastic, they are also getting trapped in it. Sea turtles have been found tangled in fishing nets, plastic twine, six-pack rings, kite string and other plastic packaging — and the deaths can be long and drawn out. Sometimes a turtle will be tangled for a year before it dies.

SEA LIONS AND SEALS

Sea lions and seals are curious, playful and wonderful animals. Studies on populations of Stellar Sea Lions in Alaska have found packaging bands for boxes, as well as ropes and abandoned fishing nets, wrapped around their necks. Researchers predict that their playful nature often leads these animals to play with plastic debris, which can lead them to get tangled, creating harmful wounds.

FISH

Some estimates have predicted that by 2050, there will be more plastic in our oceans than there are fish. The reason is because we continue to throw away more and more plastic every year, and this plastic is killing fish. The amount of plastic keeps going up, and the number of fish keeps going down. Like other animals, fish can become trapped in plastic and can eat deadly amounts of it, but a recent study found that plastic can also damage a fish's liver. Like a person's liver, a fish's liver helps filter out toxins, such as pesticides and pollutants. The more plastic a fish eats, the more it will damage its liver, so the more it will be harmed.

Whale Shark

The whale shark is the world's largest fish! They swim with their enormous mouth wide open, catching plankton, which are small organisms that float in water. This method is called filter feeding. A whale shark swallows water in one day that would be near the same as you drinking the contents of 40,000 two-liter soda bottles. In the process of swallowing so much water, filter feeders ingest a lot of microplastics. Research has shown that eating microplastics affects a whale shark's growth, reproduction and overall health. However, more research is needed to understand the problem better. Other filter feeders affected by plastic include manta rays and many whale species.

A Rubber Ducky's Journey

Another way plastic enters our oceans is when it falls overboard, off a boat! The World Shipping Council estimates that an average of 350 shipping containers are lost each year. Examples of containers lost at sea include one filled with 3 million pieces of Lego, another with 34,000 hockey gloves and another with 50,000 Nike shoes — that's a lot of plastic!

But one container stands out from all the rest. On January 10, 1992, a ship making its way from Hong Kong to Tacoma, Washington, traveled through a big storm. The ship lost 12 containers in rough waters. One of these containers held over 28,000 bathtub toys. Some of these toys were red beavers, green frogs and blue turtles, but most of them were yellow rubber ducks. Unlike many bath toys, these duckies did not have a hole in the bottom, so they were able to float without taking on water. From this point, the toys began an incredible journey.

Many of the ducks are likely still stuck in a loop close to where they fell off the ship. This loop is known as an ocean gyre — specifically in this case, the North Pacific Gyre.

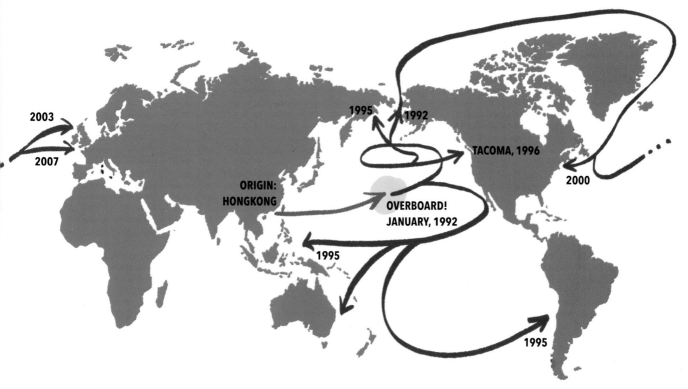

On the map:
- **2003**
- **2007**
- **1995**
- **1992**
- **TACOMA, 1996**
- **ORIGIN: HONGKONG**
- **OVERBOARD! JANUARY, 1992**
- **2000**
- **1995**
- **1995**

DESTINATION ALASKA, DESTINATION AUSTRALIA

Eight months later, hundreds of rubber ducks were being found on the shores of Sitka, Alaska — over 5,600 miles (3,500 km) from where they went overboard. This gave oceanographer Curtis Ebbesmeyer an idea. To learn about ocean currents, scientists had been releasing messages in bottles in an attempt to see where they would end up. However, sending only 1,000 or so bottles adrift meant that not many actually landed on shore. But 28,000 floating bath toys, now that was something that could be tracked! So Ebbesmeyer tracked the ducks and found that, while some went north to Alaska, others traveled south, landing in Australia, Indonesia and South America. Some eventually traveled to Japan, while still more made it to their intended destination in Washington — four years late! The map above shows the trajectory of the toys after they fell overboard.

FROZEN IN ICE

Amazingly, some of the ducks traveled even further north than Alaska. They went through the Bering Strait, which is a narrow path of water between Russia and Alaska. These ducks became frozen in sea ice and continued to travel slowly and steadily across the North Pole. The toys began to thaw and make their way into the Atlantic Ocean, and by the early 2000s, they were arriving on the East Coast of Canada. The company that manufactured the toys offered a $100 reward for each rubber duck recovered.

What is a Garbage Patch?

It would be one thing if the only human-made items floating around in ocean gyres were the bath toys from 1992. It would make for an adorable news item and a fairly simple cleanup. However, trillions (that's 1,000,000,000,000) of pieces of plastic are currently trapped in ocean gyres. A gyre is a system of circulating ocean currents that form a vortex, which is a fast-moving circle of water.

These swirling ocean waters are formed by a combination of currents, tides, temperatures and salinity (which means the level of salt in the water), as well as wind patterns. There are five main gyres:

1. **INDIAN OCEAN GYRE**
2. **NORTH ATLANTIC GYRE**
3. **NORTH PACIFIC GYRE**
4. **SOUTH ATLANTIC GYRE**
5. **SOUTH PACIFIC GYRE**

Gyres serve an important service by moving ocean waters around the planet, but they also pull waste into them, where it becomes trapped in the center of the massive swirl. These collections of waste have been nicknamed "garbage patches."

When you imagine a patch, what do you think of? Do you picture one giant mound of trash? An island you can stand on? Though garbage patches are often described this way, you cannot stand on them or see them from space. They are actually a lot more like a dark, cloudy soup, with bits and pieces floating on and just below the surface, which makes them all the more troublesome because the small fragments that make up the patch are harder to clean up and are hazardous to animals that may eat the plastic.

Scientists have found 50 plastic items in the Great Pacific Garbage Patch with production dates that they could read: one from 1977, seven from the 1980s, 17 from the 1990s, 24 from the 2000s and one from 2010.

MEGA, MACRO, MESO, MICRO

Worn by the waves and broken down by the sun's rays, plastic pieces in garbage patches are often hard to tell apart. For this reason, scientists group ocean plastics into four main types, based on their size:

NAME	SIZE	EXAMPLES
Megaplastic	Greater than 20 inches (50 cm)	Fishing nets
Macroplastic	2 to 20 inches (5 to 50 cm)	Crates and bottles
Mesoplastic	¼ to 2 inches (0.5 to 5 cm)	Bottle caps
Microplastic	1/50 to ¼ inch (0.05 to 0.5 cm)	Fragments of rigid plastic

THE GREAT PACIFIC GARBAGE PATCH

The largest and most widely researched garbage patch is the Great Pacific Garbage Patch. You won't find much wood, metal or paper in this patch — because it is 99.9% plastic! It is the largest collection of floating plastic on our planet, so maybe its nickname should be the Pacific Plastic Patch!

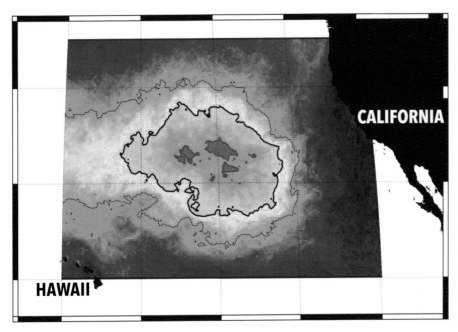

This composite image shows the location of the Great Pacific Garbage Patch. The solid line and the dotted line, respectively, denote the core of the patch and its outer reaches. The colors indicate the concentration of garbage in the patch, with red being the highest concentration. This highlights that the patch is not a solid island of garbage.

Since the patch is *not* one solid mass but rather a soup, it is difficult to measure its true size. However, scientists currently estimate it is almost 618,000 square miles (1.6 million square kilometers) — that is four times the size of Germany. About 1.8 trillion pieces make up the patch, and it has a mass of 87,000 tons (79,000 metric tons) — four times bigger than previously thought, and it's only growing!

By weight, megaplastics are the biggest contributor to the patch, but in terms of pieces, microplastics make up 94% of it. Larger pieces of mega-, macro- and mesoplastic are constantly being broken down by waves and the rays of the sun, turning them into microplastic. This is the main problem with plastic waste: It may get smaller, but it doesn't go away!

Ghost nets are the main element of the patch by weight, making up 46% of its total mass. If we are going to solve the plastic problem, the fishing industry will need to make many changes.

Microplastics

What do you consider plastic waste? Odds are, your mind will go to things that are often discarded and are easy to identify, such as straws, shopping bags and water bottles. However, one of the largest pollution problems our world faces is something no one purposely throws away and that is very, very small. That problem is microplastics. Smaller than ¼ inch (5 mm), these tiny pieces of plastic have been reported in every ocean, including the Arctic Ocean, around where very few people live. Their small size makes them easy to be ingested by even small organisms, such as zooplankton, and that size also makes this plastic incredibly hard for people to notice and clean up.

FROM BIG TO LITTLE

Plastics never fully break down, but they do break apart. Plastic in a landfill can take hundreds of years to break apart, but in the ocean it is a different story. Floating on the surface, weathered by waves and photodegraded by the sun, this plastic can start flaking apart within months! Over time, a single piece of plastic debris can break apart into a million tiny pieces.

ALWAYS LITTLE

Most microplastics enter our waterways as larger plastic pieces that break apart over time. However, a *lot* of plastic in our oceans started little and has stayed little.

Nurdles

You already know that nurdles are plastic pellets that are melted down to make almost all of the plastic we use in our daily lives. They can get lost when they are accidentally spilled at factories or when they are being transported, leading to billons of nurdles floating in the oceans.

Microbeads

Microbeads are plastic bits smaller than a 1/32 inch (1 mm) that are often added to the toothpaste and skin cleaning products we use because their rough texture helps scrub things clean. These beads replace natural products with rough textures, such as walnut husks and oatmeal. Many nations, including Australia, Canada, England, France and the United States, among others, have banned the use of microbeads in cosmetics that are routinely washed off. That's good news because when products with these beads are washed off they go down the drain and into the sewer. The waste water is treated, but the microbeads still manage to escape. As many as 27 microbeads can be found per gallon of waste water (or seven microbeads per liter). This may not sound like a lot, but when you consider the trillions of gallons of water treated every year, it really adds up!

Spin Cycle

Have you ever helped do the laundry? You may have had to clean out the dryer filter and noticed that it was full of lint. This lint is made up of little pieces of fibers that have fallen off your clothes. These pieces come off your sweaters and socks in the dryer, but they also come off in the washing machine. A shocking 700,000 synthetic fibers come off our clothes in a *single* load of laundry.

So how big a deal is this? If you lived in a city of 100,000 people, over the course of a year, your city would produce 793 pounds (360 kg) of plastic fibers just from washing your clothes! These fibers go from your machine to the sewer system, but because the fibers are so small — thinner than your hair — most of them don't get filtered out and go directly into our waterways. And the fibers made from fabric like polyester and nylon take hundreds of years to breakdown!

TINY TOXIC SPONGES

When in water, microplastics act like sponges, soaking up a lot of chemicals from the water. Their surface can become covered in contaminants called persistent bioaccumulating toxins, or PBTs for short. When animals eat these polluted bits, they end up polluting themselves! Microplastics have been found inside more than 100 different species. When ingested, these plastics release dangerous PBTs into the animal's body. So how do scientists know if an animal has eaten microplastics? One solution involves examining their poop! For example, scientists in the Arctic discovered that walruses were eating microplastics by collecting and examining their feces. It's a stinky job, but it's all done in the name of science!

Plastic Through the Food Web

You are alive! To stay alive, you need to eat food. By eating food you get nutrients, which are substances your body needs so you have energy and can learn, grow and create. But what would happen if what you thought was food wasn't actually food? What if every time you ate, there was a chance that, instead of biting into a nutritious snack, you got a piece of plastic? This happens every day to animals across the world, and it's how plastic becomes part of the food web. But what exactly is a food web?

A FOOD WEB EXPLAINED

A food web is a series of food chains that are connected to each other. A food chain is a straight path that energy from food travels along. For example, if you had salmon for dinner, then you might be part of this food chain:

ALGAE (PHYTOPLANKTON) → SHRIMP → SALMON → HUMAN

What if you also had broccoli with your salmon? You would also be part of this food chain:

BROCCOLI → HUMAN

In the salmon and broccoli dinner example, you are part of two different food chains. Chances are you eat a variety of different foods every day. For that reason, it makes more sense to represent our diets with a food web instead of a single food chain.

Below are two food webs. On the left is one you would be a part of if you ate a chicken club sandwich (one made with animals raised in a free-range, organic environment where the food they were given to eat was part of their natural diet), and on the right is another showing how a food web works in the wild.

FOOD WEB OF A CHICKEN CLUB SANDWICH

FOOD WEB IN THE WILD

PRODUCERS AND CONSUMERS

Every food web includes two groups of living things: producers and consumers. Plants do not eat food, but they do make — or produce — their own food through photosynthesis. (Photosynthesis is a process whereby plants (like the tree above) use sunlight to turn carbon dioxide and water into food for themselves.) One oceanic producer is phytoplankton. It provides the base for many of the ocean's food webs. Phytoplankton is food for shrimp, snails, jellyfish and even whales!

Consumers cannot produce their own energy, so they need to eat — or consume — food to survive. You are a consumer! So are all animals. There are different types of consumers:

Herbivores are animals that eat mainly plants. Oceanic herbivores include mussels, parrotfish and green sea turtles. Zebras, cows and deer are some examples of land herbivores.

Omnivores are animals that eat both plants and animals. Oceanic omnivores include zooplankton, snails and crabs. Apes, rats and robins are some examples of land omnivores. Humans are also omnivores.

Carnivores are animals that mainly eat other animals. Oceanic carnivores include the great white shark. Lions, wolves and hawks are some examples of land carnivores.

PHYTOPLANKTON

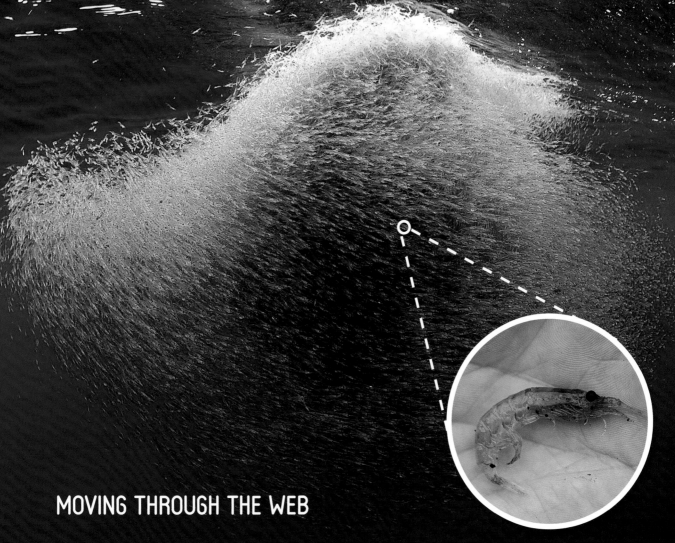

MOVING THROUGH THE WEB

What happens when an animal that has eaten plastic is then eaten by another animal?

To investigate this, let's look at filter feeders in the ocean. Filter feeders are animals that eat by straining little pieces of food out of the water. For example, mussels feed on phytoplankton and other microscopic organisms that are floating in the water.

Scientists have recently discovered that, along with food, mussels are filtering in microplastics. For every 3.5 ounces (100 grams) of mussels (about 10 mussels), scientists found 70 particles of microplastic. Mussels are also food for thousands of different animals.

Unfortunately, mussels aren't the only ones eating plastic fibers. Zooplankton (such as the krill pictured here) are tiny organisms that drift in ocean currents. They eat plastic fibers, and they are an important food source for several animals, including humpback whales. A humpback whale routinely eats 1,100 pounds (500 kg) a day of zooplankton, which means the whales are also consuming the plastic inside of the zooplankton. Scientists have calculated that a humpback whale likely consumes 300,000 microplastic particles on a daily basis.

Plastic, therefore, moves up the food web because some sea creatures eat plastic and then bigger sea creatures eat those smaller creatures. This is also an example of biomagnification (see illustration at left). Biomagnification is the phenomenon by which the amount of a substance, such as plastic, increases the higher you go up the food web.

Is There Plastic in Me?

IN AND OUT

A small study of European and Japanese men and women found plastic in the poop of all participants. As of right now, we know that we eat microplastic and we poop it out. But do we get it all out? Scientists don't know yet. They are also working to understand if the plastic we eat changes once inside us.

Chances are you do have plastic inside you. But don't panic! You are not alone. More than 700 different animal species are known to eat plastic. Some animals eat plastic when they mistake it for food — which is not something many humans do — and others get plastic inside them by eating animals that have eaten plastic. This does sometimes happen to humans. There are also other ways plastic can enter your body.

Salty Plastic

If you crack some sea salt over your dinner, chances are you are getting a little plastic with your sodium. A recent study has found that 90% of all sea salt contains microplastic. Why? Because sea salt is produced by evaporating sea water to leave only the salt. If that water contains plastic fibers, those remain along with the salt after the evaporation process. Of the 39 salt brands that scientists tested, 36 had plastic in them. It's estimated that we eat 2,000 pieces of microplastics every year just from salt!

Watered-Down Plastic

Here's a surprising statistic: 90% of bottled water contains microplastic. The most common type of plastic fragment scientists found was polypropylene, which is the same material used to make the bottle caps. The fibers could be fragments from the bottle cap, or they could be microfibers that are floating in the air and then fall inside the bottles. Truthfully, we don't know.

Scientists have also found plastic in tap water, but the concentration appears to be much higher in bottled water. The highest concentration the scientists found was more than 38,000 pieces of microplastic per gallon of water (10,000 pieces per liter of water).

Aired-Out Plastic

About 16% of the world's plastic is used in textile fibers. Our synthetic clothes release microfibers not only into the water when they are washed, but also into the air when they are dried and being worn.

A recent study found that 29% of fibers in the air are made of plastic, and we breathe those fibers into our lungs. For the most part we also breathe them right back out, which is a good thing. However, studies have found that some of these fibers remain stuck to the inside of our lungs, and if the concentration becomes high enough, it can lead to infection. For example, people who handle plastic textiles every day for work have a higher rate of lung disease.

Mealtime Plastic

If you eat mollusks, such as mussels, clams or oysters, you are likely also eating plastic. When you eat mollusks, you eat the entire organism, including its stomach, meaning you also eat everything that it ate, which often includes plastic.

When you eat fish, however, you don't eat their stomach. You only eat their muscle tissue. Current science indicates that the microplastics do not move from the stomach into muscle tissue. But there may be another way for plastic from fish to get inside you. Scientists are investigating nanoplastics — nano being even smaller than micro. These nanoplastic fibers are so fine that they are basically invisible. These tiny fibers can move through cells, including tissues and organs. The science is just starting on this topic.

Is Plastic Toxic?

The word "chemical" often makes us think of something bad, since it is associated with things such as cleaning products and pesticides (which are products used to kill bugs). But many chemicals, such as water (which is composed of two hydrogen molecules and one oxygen molecule, H_2O), are essential for life. In fact, everything around you is made of chemicals.

However, some chemicals — such as those in many household cleaners and pesticides — really are quite bad for us. And, yes, some bad chemicals are found in plastic. But what is the risk to people?

UNDERSTANDING TOXICITY

Before we can judge how risky using plastic is, we must first understand toxicity. Toxicity is the degree to which a chemical changes or damages a person's body. However, it's important to remember that, even when a chemical can damage our bodies, the amount of the chemical needed to cause damage may be much greater than the amount a person is likely to be exposed to.

A dosage is the term scientists use to indicate the average amount of a specific chemical a person can tolerate without being harmed in a significant way. In other words, more than the maximum recommended dosage could lead to poisoning, and being exposed to the chemical at those levels is toxic.

For example, chocolate contains a chemical called theobromine, which can be toxic. If you ate 85 full-size chocolate bars in a row, you

could exceed the maximum dosage of theobromine. Similarly, eating too many bananas could give you a deadly amount of potassium (which is a mineral that, in the right amounts, your body actually needs to function properly).

Even water, in large enough quantities, can poison you.

Chocolate, bananas and water are *not* bad for you, but in high enough doses nearly everything can harm you. The phrase scientists say is "the dose is the poison."

DIFFERENT PLASTIC, DIFFERENT TOXIC RISK

Different pieces of plastic are made with different ingredients. Therefore, when assessing whether a particular type of plastic is harmful, we can't treat all plastics the same. However, there are common ingredients added to many types of plastic, which are known as "plasticizers," that can be dangerous. The two additives that are most concerning are bisphenol A (BPA) and phthalates.

BPA

BPA is added to make clear, hard plastics, such as those used to make reusable water bottles. BPA is also used to make epoxy resins that line metal food containers to keep the food inside them fresher, such as a can of tuna. However, BPA can be released from the container and go into your food or drink, making it easy to injest without you even knowing it.

Even if you are just holding a plastic container, you can absorb BPA through your skin. This effect is even greater if the plastic is heated up, for example, in the microwave, or left in the sun, where it is exposed to UV rays.

Once BPA is in your body, it can imitate human hormones (hormones are molecules in your body that send important messages to your organs — they help regulate how you think and feel). In high enough doses, BPA can disrupt processes in your body that help control how you digest food, how you grow and how you sleep. Because of this potential harm, BPA is banned in some products. For example, babies can be particularly sensitive to BPA, so it has been removed from baby bottles and dishes in many parts of the world.

BPA FREE?

Concerns about the safety of BPA has led many manufacturers to start making "BPA-free" products. However, studies have found that the BPA replacements can also be dangerous. Other studies have found that *all* plastic has the potential to disrupt people's biological systems.

Phthalate

Phthalates are added to make plastic soft and flexible. They are found in PVC pipes, which are used for plumbing, in the tubes used in hospitals to deliver medications and even in the coating of some pills we take. Phthalates are also found in soda bottles (where these chemicals can move from the bottle into the drink, especially when the drink has a lot of acid, such as cola).

Like BPA, phthalates can disrupt hormone activity. Studies have linked phthalates to birth defects (which are problems in newborn babies), cancers and diabetes. In some parts of the world, phthalates are strictly regulated and are often banned in children's toys, but this is not the case everywhere.

HOT PLASTIC

Heating a Styrofoam container used for take-out food can let styrene, which is a carcinogen (meaning it can cause cancer), into your meal.

Plastic that is labeled microwave safe *will* release plasticizers, but the amount is 100 to 1,000 times less than the toxic dosage. Don't use any containers if they are scratched, cracked or stained – these are more likely to release plasticizers. When in doubt, use glass, which won't release any chemicals.

Global Issues

It's likely that when you and your family take out the trash and recycling, a truck comes by and takes it away to be processed in a waste management facility. Other than helping to sort the waste in your house and perhaps take it to the curb (or to a garbage room in your building), you probably don't have to think much more about your waste. This, however, is not the case for many people throughout the world.

Citizens in low- and middle-income nations are deeply affected by waste — both theirs and yours. Every day, two billion people — more than one-quarter of the world's population — do not have basic waste removal services. They have to rely on informal waste pickers or their own strategies, such as burning it or dumping it into rivers.

The problems associated with pollution are not experienced by all people equally or fairly. Many of the world's most vulnerable people, such as the female waste picker pictured here, are directly put into harm's way. David Attenborough, the famous British broadcaster and natural historian, has pointed out that plastic pollution is killing people. A recent study estimates that as many as 1 million people die each year from diseases and accidents related to poorly managed waste in developing nations.

BIG POLLUTERS, LITTLE RESPONSIBILITY

Between 1992 and 2018, 45% of all plastic waste was sent to China to be recycled. This included huge shipments of waste from Europe, North America and Japan. For these more wealthy countries, shipping plastic to China was often more convenient than dealing with it at home.

This all changed in January 2018, when China abruptly stopped accepting plastic waste. Other South-Asian nations, particularly Malaysia, stepped in to fill China's role, but the amount of waste being sent overseas for recycling is now lower, and a lot of plastic waste isn't being recycled at all.

In the United States, many waste management companies that were sending plastic waste to China are now sending it to American landfills. Before China stopped taking our plastic waste, it was actually a money-making business for traders to deal in plastic waste — selling bundles of desirable plastics to the highest bidder. Now the same traders have to pay people to take it. All of this means our society needs to reevaluate our strategies around recycling.

WASTE MISMANAGED

There are many ways in which waste isn't managed properly, but there are two main ones: poor waste management facilities in low- and middle-income nations, and people in developed nations using too much plastic — often called over consumption — which leads to excess waste. Turn the page to find out more.

51

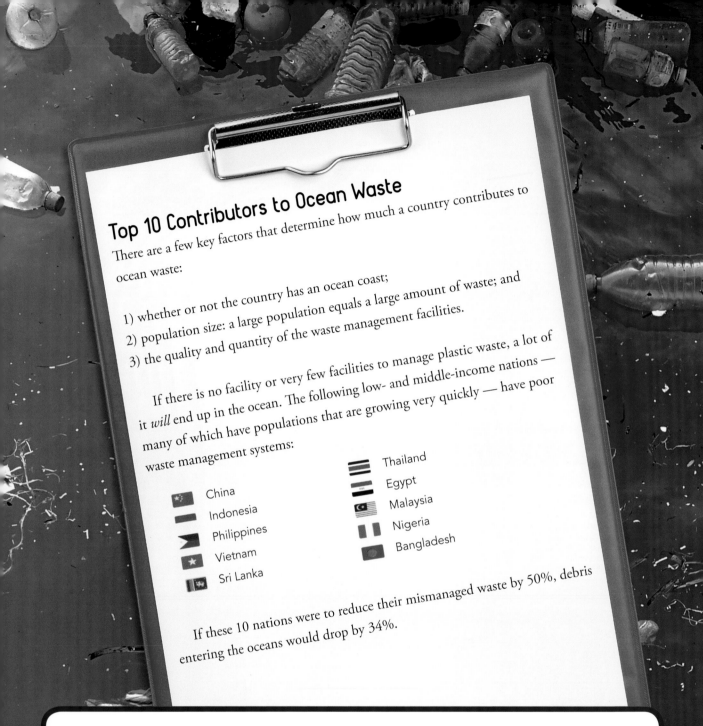

Top 10 Contributors to Ocean Waste

There are a few key factors that determine how much a country contributes to ocean waste:

1) whether or not the country has an ocean coast;

2) population size: a large population equals a large amount of waste; and

3) the quality and quantity of the waste management facilities.

If there is no facility or very few facilities to manage plastic waste, a lot of it *will* end up in the ocean. The following low- and middle-income nations — many of which have populations that are growing very quickly — have poor waste management systems:

China
Indonesia
Philippines
Vietnam
Sri Lanka

Thailand
Egypt
Malaysia
Nigeria
Bangladesh

If these 10 nations were to reduce their mismanaged waste by 50%, debris entering the oceans would drop by 34%.

A GLOBAL ISSUE, A GLOBAL SOLUTION

Unfortunately, there is no one person, country or industry to blame for the problems related to plastic. Our health and the health of our oceans depends on people and countries coming together and creating global solutions. This means that the countries with more money need to support waste management facilities in the countries that need help. It also involves reducing the amount of waste that we produce and the consumption that creates the demand for single-use plastic.

There is no *one* solution to the plastic problem; it requires many different approaches.

Waste in the World's Richest Nations

The 10 nations noted on the previous page may contribute the most waste to the world's oceans, but the citizens who live in those countries create less waste than the worldwide per-person average, which is 3.7 pounds (1.7 kg) per person per day (which equals the weight of 17 apples!). Many high-income nations are creating much more waste than that.

Below are the average pounds (and kilograms) of waste produced per person per day in seven of the richest countries in the world.

AVERAGE POUNDS (KILOGRAMS) OF WASTE PER PERSON PER DAY

Low-Income Countries	Worldwide	High-Income Countries
1.5 (0.7)	3.7 (1.7)	5 (2.3)

WASTE PRODUCED BY SEVEN OF THE WORLD'S RICHEST COUNTRIES

Nation	Average Pounds (kg) of Waste per Person per Day
United States	5.69 (2.58)
Canada	5.14 (2.33)
Italy	4.92 (2.23)
Germany	4.65 (2.11)
France	4.23 (1.92)
United Kingdom	3.95 (1.79)
Japan	3.77 (1.71)

A Global Solution: End Users

The plastic problem is a complicated global problem that does not have any borders. However, even with big problems, the best solutions sometimes start at home.

When someone buys a product and brings it home or has it delivered, they are called an "end user." This means that a product was created, marketed and distributed to stores for people to buy and use, and that those people are probably the last place that product will be used, and it will then go to a landfill. Now more than ever, it is important that we, as end users, play a role in protecting our planet.

Here are some ways end users (and the companies that provide goods to end users) are making a difference.

CONSUME LESS

Perhaps the single best thing we can do *right now* is to buy less stuff — not just plastic, but less of everything. Some reports have found that North Americans consume twice as much stuff today as they did 50 years ago, and a lot of it they don't really use. Similar changes are happening in Britain, where the average 10-year-old owns 238 toys but regularly plays with only 12. Living with less means less waste sent to landfills, less waste entering the oceans, fewer carbon

emissions from production, less wasted water (a lot of water is used to make our stuff!), less pollution and hopefully a change in perspective.

There are many examples of ways to consume fewer things. From changing their diet to living in a smaller space, people all over the world are actively trying to live with less. Here are two examples of things you can start doing today!

Wear Fewer Clothes

Clothing is one of the biggest contributors to worldwide waste. One relatively simple way to start living with less is Project 333, where for three months people limit themselves to a wardrobe of only 33 items of clothing.

In a similar experiment, Matilda Kahl decided to get rid of the headache of deciding what to wear every day and wore a "uniform" to work. Instead of owning many different items of clothing, Matilda purchased enough of the same black pants and the same white shirt to wear to work every week.

Move Toward Zero Waste

Laura Singer made headlines in 2016 by fitting all of her waste from the previous four years into one 16-ounce (473 ml) mason jar! She has inspired thousands of people around the world to join the Zero Waste Movement. The goal of Zero Waste is for no waste to be sent to landfills, incinerators or the oceans. Laura recycles and composts some waste, but otherwise practices the 6Rs that you'll learn about it in the next chapter. From makeup to coffee cups, Laura has found refillable, reusable and ecological options. Do some research and you may be amazed at what is available to you to help reduce your personal waste.

THINKING OUTSIDE THE PLASTIC BOX

How do people invent new and better ways of doing things? You might assume that you would need the latest tech or a lot of money, but that's not necessarily the case. To be inventive, all you really need is an open mind and the courage to try new ideas.

These are just few examples of simple ways people and companies are creatively trying to improve the end-user side of the plastic problem.

Skipping the Plastic Rings

Carlsberg, which is based in Denmark, is the first beer producer to replace plastic six-pack rings with glue. Yes, instead of fastening six cans together with plastic rings, Carlsberg uses a super-strong glue that connects neighboring cans to each other. This new method of putting six cans together cuts the amount of plastic used by 76% and eliminates the dreaded rings, which too often find their way to the ocean, where animals get caught in their plastic loops. This inventive idea could be used for all sorts of canned beverages.

Taking the Waste Out of Takeout

Every day, millions of people order food cooked at a restaurant that they then pick up and take home or have delivered. Typically, an order comes with a lot of waste, which may include plastic forks and knives and a bunch of ketchup packets. To limit this waste, some online food ordering services have included an option at the checkout to select "skip the utensils." In one year, giving consumers this option saved American take-out food delivery company, Seamless, over 1 million napkins and utensils! Next time you order in, tell them "skip the utensils!"

Ghost-Net Carpets

Abandoned fishing gear produces a lot of waste and kills thousands of animals every year. To help solve this problem, communities across the Philippines and Cameroon, with the help of the Net-Works Foundation, are converting recovered fishing gear into carpets. Over 220 tons (200 metric tons) of nets have been collected, often by fishers who are out of work due to declining fish populations. They've collected enough plastic to wrap around the world's equator four times! The nets are then recycled into nylon yarn, which is then sold and woven into carpet tiles.

Turning Bottles into Schools

What if you could turn a candy wrapper into a classroom? That is what is happening in Guatemala, through the organization Hug It Forward. Working with local communities that do not have waste management facilities, they help collect plastic bottles and other discarded containers and fill them with pieces of non-perishable trash to create "eco-bricks," which are used to build schools! Since 2009, this program has helped build over 100 schools.

WHY WE CAN'T COMPLETELY BAN PLASTIC

A plastic straw is used for a few minutes before being tossed in the trash, where it will last, like most plastic, for 1,000 years and possibly end up somewhere it was never meant to be — like in the nose of a sea turtle. In 2018, prompted by a viral video of a turtle injured by a straw, people around the world grew anxious about plastic straw waste. Since then, companies — including McDonalds and Starbucks — have announced that they will gradually stop offering plastic straws in their restaurants. Even cities are banning straws: As of July 2018, Seattle is the largest U.S. city to ban plastic straws.

There are about 8.3 billion plastic straws on beaches. However, straws make up only 0.025% of the total waste that enters the oceans each year. For this reason, some argue that a straw ban misses the point and takes the focus away from issues like better waste management. Others argue that the straw ban is an awesome first step that encourages people to think about their use of plastic, which can motivate them to make even more positive changes.

Banning plastic is a complicated issue. Here's why:

"Green" Options Aren't Always Better

A reusable canvas bag might seem to be a much more environmentally friendly option compared to a plastic bag. However, when it comes to climate change, one study found that canvas bags contribute more to global warming than plastic bags because their production and distribution require so much energy and resources.

For example, reusing a single-use plastic grocery bag three times has the same carbon footprint as using a cotton tote bag 393 times. Similarly, you can compare two T-shirts, one made of cotton and one made of polyester (which are plastic fibers): A polyester shirt requires 568 gallons (2,150 liters) less water to produce than its cotton counterpart — 92 gallons (350 liters) versus 660 gallons (2,500 liters).

This book has a plastic laminated cover. Adding a plastic coating to the cover paper keeps the cover from ripping and enables it to last much, much longer.

Non-plastic Alternatives Are Often Heavier

The plastic used in modern cars makes them lighter and more fuel-efficient than older cars, meaning we use less gas to get around. It's also much lighter to ship plastic goods than those made of glass. For example, if you were to ship two boxes by truck from Montreal to Detroit, each with 50 jugs of juice in them — one box full of 1 quart (1 liter) glass jugs and the other full of 1 quart PET jugs — the plastic jugs would use about ¾ ounce (22 g) of CO_2 per jug less than the glass jugs. That equals an overall savings of more than two bathtubs full of CO_2 per box! However, most companies don't just send one box of goods; they send hundreds or thousands of them. It's something worth considering.

Plastic Can Help Reduce Food Waste

Food waste is another important environmental challenge. One-third of all food is never eaten and is simply thrown out! Today, many argue that plastic packaging helps keep food from spoiling, so the food is eaten rather than thrown out. However, others argue that plastic packaging encourages us to buy more than we need. For example, instead of buying the four potatoes needed to make a potato salad, many will buy the 5-pound (2.5 kg) bag instead. Since it is more than they need, it can lead to a cupboard full of rotting potatoes!

Plastic Is Essential in Some Industries

Health care, for example, has been completely transformed by plastics, which have been used to create affordable and safe options for doctors and hospitals. From machines and laboratory equipment to artificial body parts and contact lenses, plastics have helped reduce medical costs, reduce the rates of infectious diseases, bring medicine to hard-to-get-to places and make patients feel better.

THE CASE FOR LIMITING PLASTIC BAGS

We know that single-use plastic bags threaten ocean wildlife, tricking many animals into thinking they are food. Also, these bags are often not recyclable. This has led over 30 countries to ban them entirely. For example, in 2017 Kenya began one of the world's strictest plastic bag bans, including fines and even prison sentences for people and businesses who were found using them. This has significantly reduced the amount of trash on the streets, which is important because mosquitos often breed in water that pools in plastic trash, and these insects can carry malaria, which is a deadly disease.

Another tactic to reduce the use of plastic bags is to charge a tax on them. A study across California found that if grocery stores offer a plastic bag for free, 75% of people will say "yes please!" and take the bag. When stores charged as little as 10 cents per bag, that figure dropped to 16% of shoppers. In Denmark, a plastic bag costs 50 cents — significantly higher than many bag fees around the world — and this has led most Danes to use only four bags per year. By comparison, Americans use on average one bag per day (or 365 bags per year).

The 6Rs

You've probably heard of the 3Rs: reduce, reuse and recycle. But have you heard of the 6Rs: reduce, reuse, repair, refuse, rethink and recycle? With the large amount of plastic in our lives today, it is more important than ever for each of us to limit our waste. Repair, refuse and rethink are important ideas for all of us to adopt. Below is a list of how you and your family can use the 6Rs to help you fight unnecessary waste.

Reduce

Reduce means to make a smaller amount of waste. Here are some ways to accomplish it:

- **Buy less stuff:** We often buy more things than we actually need. The next time you are tempted to ask for a new toy or pair of shoes, take some time to think about it. Do you still want it after 20 minutes? Do you still want it after 30 days? Instead of asking for something new, could you share with a neighbor or friend?

- **Choose less packaging:** When your parents are choosing products, do they consider the packaging? Do you? When your parents are grocery shopping, or when you are buying a new toy, could you or your parents switch the product you are buying for one that uses less plastic? Could you buy a product without any packaging at all? Find out if there is a store in your community where people can bring their own reusable containers and fill them with the things they need, such as pasta, nuts and grains.

BIGGER IS (SOMETIMES) BETTER

Purchasing in large quantities can reduce the amount of packaging waste. For example, in this picture it takes four containers to reach the same volume as this one container,  but the four containers make double the waste. This is due to the surface area to volume ratio, which is the relationship between an object's volume (how much it can hold) and its surface area. However, it is recommended that people only buy everyday things in bulk — such as liquid hand soap — so they don't end up throwing things out, creating more waste.

Reuse

Instead of throwing something away after one use, why not reuse it!

- **Repurpose old containers:** When your family is done using a container, try to use it for something else. For example, an empty container of yogurt could be used to store your crayons. A container used for mints could store your headphones. You could grow a plant inside an old ice cream container. You could turn a juice jug into a bird feeder.
- **Skip single-use plastic:** Having a party? Why not ask your parents to skip the plastic and go with reusable plates and cutlery instead? You can volunteer to do the dishes! Going out for a hot chocolate? Bring a reusable mug! Going to the store? Bring your reusable bag! Going to play soccer? Bring your reusable water bottle!
- **One person's trash could be someone else's treasure:** When you need new clothes, why not ask your mom or dad to take a look in a secondhand store? If you have outgrown clothes that are still in good shape, you can ask your parents to donate them, sell them or give them to one of your friends. Consider asking your parents to host a "free market" or a clothing swap. This is an event where people gather up things they no longer need or want so other people can take them for free — invite your neighbors and friends!

Rethink

When we look at single-use plastic, we often only see it as trash, but it doesn't have to be that way! Rethink how you value plastic:

- **Musical plastic:** Artist Shady Rabab has been teaching kids how to turn plastic bottles into amazing musical instruments.
- **Plastic is strong:** Designer Micaella Pedros is making furniture using scrap wood and plastic bottles found as litter. By heating the plastic around two pieces of wood, it forms an extra strong and stable joint.
- **Make something new:** The company Precious Plastic has instructions on their website that show you how to build simple machines to recycle your own plastic! One machine shreds the plastic into flakes, and another can push the plastic into molds. Since thermoplastic will melt at certain temperatures, you can turn plastic into basically anything you can imagine!

Repair

Not too long ago, people generally tried to repair something when it broke, but today we're more likely to just throw it away. Let's change that! Is there a rip in your jeans? Learn to sew a patch on it (there are thousands of online tutorials and books on how to sew). Did you break a toy? Learn how to put it back together. In your community, there may even be a "repair café," where expert volunteers will help you repair your stuff and teach you how to do it!

Refuse

A lot of useless waste is created because we're handed it, assuming we want it. You can refuse a straw, a bag, a throw-away cup — politely, of course! When you go shopping, bring your own bags. If there are stores and restaurants that your family often visits, ask your parents if you can chat to the owners about plastic. Would they be willing to only give a bag if the customer asks for it? Talking to people can lead to important changes.

Make a list of the ways you are going to add the 6Rs to your life. Let your family and friends know your plan – their support can help you commit or, better yet, you can all join in together!

Recycle

Recycling is an important piece of the puzzle, but there is a reason it is last in this list. Only 9% of all plastic is recycled. Several reasons for this are discussed on page 19, and another reason is that plastics are one of the hardest materials to recycle. There are dozens of types of plastics in everyday use, and these must be separated before they can be recycled. Afterward, bunches of sorted plastic are sent to a recycling facility to be further washed and cleaned. This is where the process gets much trickier.

Take a plastic water bottle, which is typically made of PET, one of the more valuable types of plastic. When the bottles arrive at the recycling plant, they are washed and dunked in chemicals to get the labels off, and then they are chopped into bits. The bits are then floated in a pool to separate the lid plastic from the bottle plastic. The final step is to extrude the bits — or melt them down into pellets. The pellets are then sold to manufacturers, who use them to make new products. However, all of this requires energy, and this process can release harmful chemicals into the air due to the additives that are in the plastic. Recycling is good, but far from perfect.

WHAT ABOUT BIODEGRADABLE PLASTIC?

Biodegradation is nature's way of managing waste. Microorganisms break apart food and other things, turning them into nutrients (which are substances that keep plants and animals healthy, such as vitamins and minerals).

This is one of the biggest obstacles concerning plastic waste — plastic does not easily degrade, and it's almost impossible to destroy it! That's why environmentally friendly plastics seem like such an important development. Unfortunately, it's not so simple. Let's learn about the two main green plastics on the market: biodegradable plastic and bioplastic.

Biodegradable Plastic

This type of plastic is similar to the plastic you know from your everyday life. It's made from fossil fuels, such as oil and natural gas, but it also contains additives that help the plastic break down more quickly when it is exposed to light and oxygen. These additives, however, may not always degrade the plastic. Sometimes they just turn it into smaller pieces of microplastic, which — you now know — is also a huge problem! These additives can also leave behind a toxic residue, so the plastics cannot be safely composted. The addition of these chemicals also means the plastics aren't recyclable at most facilities. For these reasons, the best place to dispose of biodegradable plastics is in a landfill. Sadly, they won't receive much light or oxygen there, and researchers have found they may not biodegrade any more easily or quickly than regular plastic.

Bioplastic

Bioplastics, on the other hand, are made by taking polymers from plants such as corn, sugarcane and wheat. Depending on how they are made, some bioplastics will break down easily in a compost bin, while others need some help. For example, many types of bioplastics need to be heated to temperatures above 135°F (57°C) for 12 weeks before they will begin to break down. This can create problems, since most recycling companies do not have the equipment needed to manage this type of plastic. As with biodegradable plastics, a lot of bioplastics end up in landfills.

New bioplastics that do not require heat to breakdown and can even be eaten are being developed. However, the single best thing we can do is to reduce the amount of waste we create!

NOT ALL RECYCLING IS CREATED EQUAL

The recycling of some materials has done a lot to help fight climate change. For example, paper and cardboard are made from raw materials such as wood. Recycling these items can save money and trees! Glass and metals, such as aluminum, can also be broken down many, many times, and their quality will stay the same.

Plastic, however, is a different story. Every time plastic is recycled, the chain of polymers that made the original item becomes shorter. Once plastic is recycled two or three times, the chain of polymers is so short it becomes almost unusable. Therefore, recycled plastic is almost always turned into a lower-grade plastic. As a comparison, a recycled aluminum can quite easily be turned back into a can, whereas it is much more difficult to turn a plastic food container back into a food container.

None of this is to say you should stop recycling! Please keep recycling. Just understand that it is only one small part of the solution.

A Global Solution: Government and Big Business

If we are going to solve the plastic problem, it is going to require the cooperation of all the world's nations as well as big businesses. Getting all of these players around the world to cooperate and commit to a problem can feel impossible — but it's not. We've solved environmental crises before!

THE OZONE LAYER

A good example of the world working together to solve an environmental crisis happened in 1985, after scientists found a huge hole in the ozone layer.

The ozone layer is an invisible layer of gas between the Earth and the sun. Our planet needs the sun for light and warmth, but the sun also gives off rays that can hurt us. The ozone layer protects us from these rays.

The hole in the ozone layer was caused by human-made chemicals, such as chlorofluorocarbons, or CFCs for short, which were found in the aerosol cans used for hairspray and air fresheners, among other products. The CFCs from these cans were flying up into the air and destroying the ozone layer.

Thankfully, in August of 1987 — within two years of the discovery of the hole — the Montreal Protocol was accepted by all 197 countries in the United Nations. This international treaty was designed to protect the ozone layer and phase out the chemicals that were destroying it.

Today, the hole has shrunk a lot, and it's expected to disappear by 2060. The lesson here is that huge environmental problems like pollution from plastic can be solved if we work together.

TIDE TURNERS

Today, as you read this, there are some remarkable efforts taking place around the world, and people everywhere are providing hope and inspiration in our fight against the plastic problem. These are just a few examples.

Cleaning Up the Great Pacific Garbage Patch

The Ocean Cleanup is an organization led by 24-year-old Boyan Slat. He and a team of scientists have created a device to remove plastic from the Great Pacific Garbage Patch. Their goal is to remove 50% of the waste from the patch by 2023! The device (pictured here on a test deployment) is a giant, flexible tube that floats on the water with a large screen that hangs from the tube below the surface of the water. Currents push the device throughout the patch as it corrals garbage. The floating tube traps large plastic waste on the surface, while the skirt traps smaller particles floating under water.

Mr. Trash Wheel and Professor Trash Wheel

As discussed on page 21, about half of all trash that enters the oceans travels through rivers. Wouldn't it be nice if a machine could collect the trash at the base of the river, so it never made it to the ocean? That is exactly what is happening in Baltimore Harbor, thanks to Mr. Trash Wheel (pictured here) and Professor Trash Wheel. Together, this dynamic duo has collected 999 tons (906 metric tons) of trash since May 9, 2014. This includes:

- 753,099 plastic bottles
- 920,154 polystyrene containers
- 10,947,000 cigarette butts
- 581,204 grocery bags
- 973,861 chip bags

How do these machines work? They are powered by the river's current, which turns a wheel that powers a belt that lifts the trash out of the water. When the current isn't strong enough, the machines are powered by the sun, using solar panels. The trash is moved along a conveyor belt and into a dumpster. Imagine if there was a Trash Wheel cleaning up every major river!

Loop Closes the Loop

Another innovative idea comes from a new company, called Loop. Loop has partnered with several brands to bring back the "milkman" model to distribute products that can be consumed. For example, instead of going to the store to buy a product in a single-use plastic bottle, such as shampoo, the product is delivered directly to the consumer in a reusable container. When the shampoo bottle is empty, the container is picked up from the person's home, washed and refilled! Loop is proposing this same system for a bunch of products, including ice cream, olive oil and laundry detergent.

Taking the Pledge

Through a collaboration between the United Nations and the Ellen MacArthur Foundation, 250 companies around the world are committing to reducing their plastic waste and pollution. These companies, including PepsiCo, Coca-Cola, Unilever, Colgate, SC Johnson and H&M, are responsible for 20% of all plastic packaging made in the world. This effort, called the New Plastics Economy, involves finding ways to reuse and repurpose plastic, avoiding single-use plastic packaging and building and improving waste collection facilities. Its ultimate goal is to find a way to close the loop on plastic waste. For more on closing the loop, turn the page.

CLOSING THE LOOP OF A LINEAR ECONOMY

A total of 91% of the world's economy is linear. But what does that mean? It means that most goods follow a straight line from beginning to end. Products are made from new resources and then dumped as waste into a landfill, an incinerator or the environment.

For example, when a new model for a phone is released, many will toss their old phone away and get the new model. When a blender is broken, most do not have it repaired — they just buy a new one.

This diagram breaks down the steps of the "take-make-waste" linear economy as it applies to the linear path of a plastic water bottle.

1. A resource is taken: Fossil fuels are taken out of the ground.
2. A product is made: Chemicals are added to the gas to turn it into the polymers that are used to make bottles. The plastic is molded into the shape of a bottle and filled with water
3. The product is distributed: Cases of water are transported around the world, sometimes traveling thousands of miles. They travel by plane, by ship and by truck and arrive in stores, where people can buy them.
4. The product is used: You buy the water bottle and drink the water.
5. The product is thrown away: You throw the empty water bottle into the trash.

This is the pattern that almost all goods follow, but it is based on two flawed assumptions:

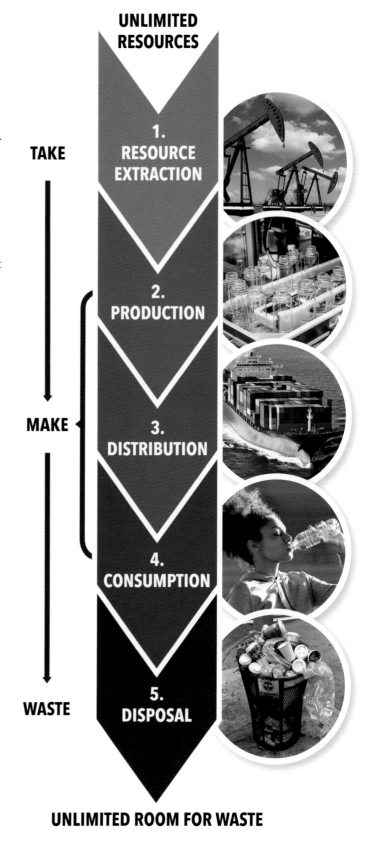

UNLIMITED RESOURCES

TAKE

1. RESOURCE EXTRACTION

2. PRODUCTION

MAKE

3. DISTRIBUTION

4. CONSUMPTION

WASTE

5. DISPOSAL

UNLIMITED ROOM FOR WASTE

Assumption 1:
THERE ARE UNLIMITED RESOURCES

Creating all goods from new resources assumes that the resources used to make the goods will never run out. This, however, is not the case! The fossil fuels that are used to make plastic are non-renewable, meaning they will eventually run out.

Assumption 2:
THERE IS UNLIMITED ROOM FOR WASTE

Throwing away goods and packaging immediately after using them assumes there is an endless amount of space where we can store the waste. This is also untrue! We are running out of space for trash. The United States alone has over 2,000 active landfills which are estimated to be full in less than 20 years!

IS LINEAR METHOD CHEAPER?

Currently, it is possible to make a water bottle from 100% recycled plastic. However, some calculations find that it costs more money to make a water bottle from recycled plastic than it does to make a bottle from new plastic. The problem is those calculations do not take into account the hidden environmental costs of making new plastic.

For example, taking fossil fuels out of the ground and burning them contributes to climate change. From the damages caused by storms to the loss of crops, climate change costs the world's economies trillions of dollars.

Similarly, buying a new product instead of fixing the old one may make the seller more money, but it does not include the hidden cost of sending the old item to a landfill or, worse, the ocean.

The Circular Economy

Luckily, it is possible to turn this line into a loop! The circular economy is a system in which resources are used for as long as possible. This process involves using the 6Rs on a global scale. However, a circular economy only works if it is applied from the very beginning of the process. In other words, businesses need to take responsibility for their products right from the start.

One example of a business closing the loop comes from IKEA. Instead of throwing out your old Ikea furniture, the store will buy it back from you and sell it secondhand or donate it to those who need it. Loop, discussed on page 69, is another example of a circular economy.

Another way for businesses to take responsibility for their products is through a polluter-pay model. In many parts of the world, people pay taxes to the government, and the government pays for the cost of recycling things. However, many are considering switching to a system in which companies pay for the recycling costs instead. Here's the idea: If companies have to pay to get rid of their products' packaging, they will be motivated to create goods with less packaging.

Reinvent the Future

When we look at the future of the plastic problem, there are reasons to be worried. Scientists predict that if we keep using plastic the way we are today, by 2050 there will be more plastic in the ocean than there are fish.

However, there are also many reasons to be optimistic. For a start, awareness about plastic pollution is growing. More people are writing about plastic, reading about plastic and learning about plastic than ever before! People like you!

Did you know that in 2018, the Collins dictionary voted "single-use" as the word of the year? This term — used to describe any product that is made to be used only once and then thrown away — was mentioned four times more often in 2018 than in the five previous years. Yes, the plastic problem is big and scary, but you can make a difference! Here are some ideas to get you started.

Organize a Cleanup and a Brand Audit

Organize a cleanup at your school or in your community! You could clean a park, a field or a shoreline. When collecting waste, do an audit of what you collect. Note the types of waste you find and, if the brand name is still visible, keep a tally of the brands you see the most. Audits like this can call attention to the companies who are regularly adding plastic pollution to the environment. You can reach out to these companies and ask them to do better!

Take pictures of your cleanup site before and after, and ask your parents if you can share the photos online. Inspiring others is one of the most important things you can do to make a difference.

Contact Your Government

Your voice matters — contact your government representatives and let them know about ways they can fight plastic pollution! Whether you contact your mayor or the leader of your country, these acts can help change things for the better. In 2013, two teenage sisters, Melati and Isabel Wijsen, from Bali, Indonesia, convinced their governor to ban plastic bags by organizing protests and demonstrations. They now run the organization, Bye Bye Plastic Bags.

Alert the Press!

Sending a letter to the editor of your local newspaper is an excellent way to share information about plastic pollution with people in your community. You can also write to magazines or post on social media (just ask your parents before going online). There are thousands of social media accounts dedicated to reducing plastic pollution and inspiring people to make changes.

Learn More

Around the world, researchers, individuals, organizations and communities are tackling the plastic problem. New studies come out all the time as we learn more about the severity of the plastic problem and find new ways to solve it. Keep up-to-date! Keep searching for new studies, events and projects.

Share What You Know (Share This Book!)

Now that you've read this book, you know a lot more about plastic than many people. Share what you know! Give a presentation at your school or to a community group. Create an event that brings attention to the plastic problem. With your parent's permission, consider making a YouTube video to share what you know. When you are done reading this book, pass it on! If you can't find it at your library, ask them to get it. The more people who learn about plastic, the better our future will be!

GLOSSARY

ALGAE A plant that grows in water and has no stem, roots or leaves. Algae is an important source of food for many marine animals. It is part of a broader family of phytoplankton.

BACTERIA A very small living organism, too small to see with just your eyes, that is found everywhere. Some are dangerous and some are helpful.

BIODEGRADATION A biological process that breaks down or decays things. Bacteria, fungi and other organisms can help this process along.

BIOMAGNIFICATION The process where-by toxins move up the food chain and become more concentrated.

CARBON DIOXIDE A gas molecule that contains one carbon atom and two oxygen atoms. When you breathe out, you are exhaling carbon dioxide. Plants absorb carbon dioxide, and it is an important part of photosynthesis.

CARBON EMISSION The process by which carbon dioxide is released into the environment by the combustion of green house gasses. The combustion of gasoline used to drive a car creates carbon emissions.

CELLULOID A type of plastic that is partly made from plant cellulose. Celluloid was often used for the film used to shoot movies.

CELLULOSE A type of carbohydrate that makes up the cell walls of plants. Cellulose is not digestible by humans but is digestible by some animals, such as cows. Cellulose is strong and flexible, and it is one of the building blocks of wood, so it is an important part of paper production.

CLIMATE CHANGE A change in climate patterns on a large scale. Climate change often refers to the increasing levels of carbon in the atmosphere, as a result of people's use of fossil fuels.

CONTAMINANT A substance that has a negative effect on an organism. Contaminants can be found in the air, water, soil and our food.

CURRENT The direction in which water flows. Currents are affected by several forces, including the rotation of the Earth, the temperature of the wind, the saltiness of the water and the gravitation of the moon!

DECOMPOSITION The process by which things break down or decay; for example, a leaf *decomposes into dirt.*

DENSITY The relationship between how much space an object takes up (its volume) and how much it weighs (its mass).

EXTINCT When an entire species is no longer living.

FRACKING A process that is used to remove oil and gas from rocks in the ground. It is done by injecting liquids at high pressures into the rocks.

GREEN Obviously a color, but also a term used to describe something that is considered environmentally friendly. However, people don't always agree about what is and isn't "environmentally friendly."

GREENHOUSE GAS A type of gas that traps the energy from the sun. These gases are related to industrial activities, such as burning coal for energy, and contribute to climate change. Carbon dioxide is an example of a *greenhouse gas.*

GYRE A large system of water that moves in a circle. They are usually found in oceans and caused by wind.

INDICATOR Any unit of measure that helps us understand what is going on in the environment.

LANDFILL A pit filled with waste. When full, these pits are often covered with dirt and plants.

LEACHATE A liquid that has traveled through a landfill. As it passes through the landfill, leachate can collect pieces of matter and chemical contaminants, which it then carries with it as it drains out of the landfill site.

MALNOURISHED When a person or animal isn't getting what they need to eat to be healthy.

MASS PRODUCTION When something is made in very large amounts. Most plastic goods are mass-produced.

MICROFIBER A very thin piece of plastic fiber — anything thinner than $\frac{2}{1,000}$ inch (0.06 mm).

MICROORGANISM A living thing that is too small to be seen with the naked eye.

MOLECULE One small unit of a substance; an example is one molecule of water.

NEUROTOXIN A poison that affects the nervous system. Your nervous system is how your brain sends and receives information about your body.

ORGANIC MATTER Matter that is made of carbon, including the decomposing animals and plants that make up soil.

PERSISTENT BIOACCUMULATING TOXIN/ PERSISTENT ORGANIC POLLUTANT A type of compound that is toxic and able to stay in the environment for a long time.

PHENOL A type of organic compound that can be taken out of coal or petroleum.

PHOTODEGRADE The process whereby an object is broken down by sunlight.

PHYTOPLANKTON Oceanic organisms that produce energy from the sun. Phytoplankton are the basis for the ocean's food webs.

POLYACTIC ACID A type of biodegradable plastic that is made from renewable resources, such as sugarcane.

POLYETHYLENE A type of polymer that is used to make many plastic products.

POLYESTER A type of fabric made of polymers.

POLYMERIZATION A chemical reaction that combines molecules so that they become larger molecules. For example, monomers combine and create polymers.

POLYPROPYLENE A polymer that is used in many types of plastic.

POLYSTYRENE A polymer that is used to make many types of plastic, including Styrofoam.

REFINED A process that removes unwanted substances; for example, refining oil removes the substances that the manufacturer does not want to keep in the oil.

RENEWABLE RESOURCE Any material that can be replaced with the passage of time; for example, wood is renewable because we can plant more trees to create more wood.

SINGLE USE A system whereby an item is used once and then thrown out or destroyed.

SULFIDE A compound made of sulfur, which is a chemical element.

SYNTHETIC A material that does not occur in nature; synthetic materials are created by people.

THERMOPLASTIC A plastic that melts when heated.

THERMOSET A plastic that does not melt when heated.

TOXIN A substance that can hurt people, animals, plants or other things in nature.

UV RAY An abbreviation for ultraviolet rays, which are waves that come from the sun and certain types of lights.

WASTE MANAGEMENT FACILITY A facility where waste is sorted and diverted. Waste may be recycled, composted, incinerated or dumped in a landfill.

WASTE PICKER People who collect reusable and recyclable material that would otherwise be thrown away. Pickers sell this material or keep it for themselves. There are millions of waste pickers throughout the world.

ZOOPLANKTON An aquatic organism that is often quite small that drifts in ocean currents. Along with phytoplankton, zooplankton makes up the majority of the ocean's food supply.

INDEX

PHOTO CREDITS

About the cover: The image for this cover is a photo compilation. Its purpose is to dramatically capture the true impact of our plastic problem. The image of the seal was taken on a different beach from the one shown. However, the plastic waste on the beach is real. (For more on this subject, see page 22.) The plastic bottle in the seal's mouth has also been added. However, it is well documented that seals and sea lions routinely play with our plastic waste and often wind up eating it or getting stuck in it. (For more on this subject, see page 30.)